blendable
curves

STACK, SLICE & SEW UNIQUE QUILTS IN A WEEKEND

PEGGY J. BARKLE

C&T PUBLISHING

Text copyright © 2007 by Peggy J. Barkle

Artwork copyright © 2007 by C&T Publishing, Inc.

Publisher: Amy Marson

Editorial Director: Gailen Runge

Acquisitions Editor: Jan Grigsby

Editor: Kesel Wilson

Technical Editors: Gayl Gallagher, Nanette S. Zeller, Teresa Stroin, and Carolyn Aune

Copyeditor/Proofreader: Wordfirm Inc.

Cover Designer: Christina Jarumay

Design Director/Book Designer: Kristy K. Zacharias

Illustrators: John Heish and Tim Manibusan

Production Coordinator: Zinnia Heinzmann

Photography by C&T Publishing, Inc., unless otherwise noted

Published by C&T Publishing, Inc., P.O. Box 1456, Lafayette, CA 94549

Library of Congress Cataloging-in-Publication Data

Barkle, Peggy J.

  Blendable curves : stack, slice & sew unique quilts in a weekend / Peggy J. Barkle.

    p. cm.

  ISBN-13: 978-1-57120-425-7 (paper trade : alk. paper)

  ISBN-10: 1-57120-425-3 (paper trade : alk. paper)

  1. Quilting--Patterns 2. Patchwork quilts--Patterns. I. Title.

  TT835.B266525 2007

  746.46--dc22

                    2006101968

Printed in China

10 9 8 7 6 5 4 3 2 1

dedication

To my parents, Wilton and Dottie Smith. Without you, I would not have made this incredible journey.

To my husband, Ken, for your incredible support, patience, love, and understanding. Without you, this book would not have become a reality.

To my children, Ryan and Katie. You will always be what I am most proud of.

To my grandmother, Iva Herrick. I miss you every day! You taught me to love without hesitation and judgment, and I strive to live by those lessons every day.

To every mother, father, sister, brother, child, and friend of a quilter. The understanding and patience you extend are precious gifts that support our passion to express who we are, who we want to be, and our relationship to the world and those important to us.

acknowledgments

I named my business *A Collective Effort Quilting Service* because I believe that none of us makes it through this life without the collective effort and support of many people we know, many we have yet to meet, and some we will never meet. People can influence us in subtle and unexpected ways, and this influence can transform our way of looking at the world.

I extend my gratitude and appreciation to Joan Meyberg and Ladye Buckner of the *Stitch 'N Quilt Shoppe* in Lawrenceville, Georgia; Annie Woods of the *Quiltmaker's Workshop* in Birmingham, Alabama, and my "Alabama Angels"; and Gail Brandt of *A Quilted Cottage* in West Jefferson, North Carolina.

Thanks also to Sandy Stites for the blessing of your friendship and expertise; to Kim Cipro for standing by my side through the best and worst of it and for truly being a girl's best friend, in this lifetime and in the next; to Kristie Michalowski for helping me take the first bite out of the apple; to Ann Ewald and Adele Steele for your support and encouragement; and to Joyce Becker for setting such a wonderful example. Friendships are an amazing gift!

Thank you to Amy Marson for your warm welcome to the C&T family; to Jan Grigsby for loving what you do; to Kesel Wilson, my editor and right hand; to Teresa Stroin, my technical editor; to Diane Pedersen, my photographer; and to all the C&T support staff who worked so enthusiastically and professionally on my behalf to bring this book to life.

contents

n • easy
nal • one
kind cre-
ve visions
e to stray
nspirations
able curve
ative voice
confidence
ress • high-
cess • color
e the lines

introduction

ets origi-
y limited
by your
gination
n • easy
al • one-
-a-kind •
e visions
urage to
inspira-
lendable
e creative
confidence
ress • high-
ss • imagine

In 2003, I was asked to develop a workshop for a quilting retreat. The guidelines I set for myself were to create a project that was fun and easy and could be completed by the time the retreat was over, but the most important guideline was that the project be something original yet familiar at the same time.

My solution to this creative challenge was to create traditional blocks with free-form curves. The curves lend a modern, abstract character to the blocks, and because each curve contains both convex and concave portions, this technique makes each quilt uniquely one-of-a-kind and fantastically original. As an extra bonus, because the blocks need to be large enough that the curve is not lost visually within the design, a quilt can be created quickly from a minimum number of blocks. How much easier could designing an art quilt be?

I believe we all carry within us creative visions that sometimes just need permission to come to life. When first learning to quilt, we naturally focus all our energy on following the correct piecing techniques for traditional patchwork. These techniques can be the building blocks for exploring all kinds of quilting. They can be the platform from which to jump toward our more creative visions and inspirations. For most of us, finding the courage to stray from the norm can be a little intimidating and overwhelming. My goal in writing this book and in developing the Blendable Curves technique is to create a bridge between the traditional and the nontraditional, a bridge to aid you in the journey to finding your own creative voice

I have structured the projects in this book to gradually introduce new elements of the technique so you can gain confidence in cutting and piecing the curves. I also show you step-by-step how to manipulate the concave areas of the curve so that sewing is a low-stress, high-success process. Best of all, I designed the projects so that everything is squared up just prior to piecing, meaning that little accuracy is required while you are piecing the traditional blocks together.

I hope you will find this book to be much more than just the patterns within it. I hope it inspires you to color outside the lines. If you have ever wanted to stray from strictly geometric patterns and create quilts that are uniquely yours but you did not know where to start, start here. Come on this journey with me and create your own original quilts using what is already familiar to you: the beautiful traditional blocks you've been sewing for years. Let's explore curves in quilting; tradition meets originality.

Remember, you are limited only by your imagination!

creating the
blendable curve

1. Stack   2. Slice   3. Shuffle   4. Sew

SIZE MATTERS

Blocks that will contain a Blendable Curve need to be made larger than the final desired size to compensate for the size loss from cutting and sewing the curve. The rule of thumb is to make the block 1″ larger in both *length* and *width*; but be aware that if the curve is cut too deeply, the loss may be more than the average 1″.

Finished block sizes need to be at least 4″ × 4″ because fitting both a concave and a convex curve in a smaller block would be difficult. The beauty of this technique is that you will be working with large blocks, and large blocks make for quick quilts. How much better could this get?

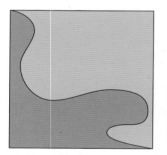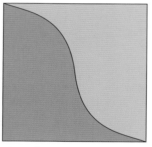

A Blendable Curve cut too deeply and a curve cut correctly

Try making a few practice squares to test your cutting and piecing tolerances. If you consistently lose more than one inch, increase the block size until it will accommodate your style of curve. If the blocks do not piece to the size anticipated, simply square up the blocks to the size of your smallest block. Your final quilt will just be a little smaller than you originally planned. No lemons at this stand—only lemonade!

1. For each curve cut, add 1″ to both the length and the width of the final desired block size.

2. Make sure the finished block size will be at least 4″ × 4″.

THE CURVE

Until now, most of us have only experienced curves like those found in the Drunkard's Path block. These blocks are pieced together from two halves, one containing a concave curve and one containing a convex curve. They need to be pinned and pieced accurately. In fact, many techniques and a special machine foot have been created to address this very issue.

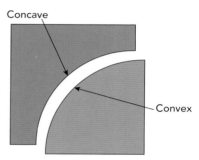

The Drunkard's Path curve

Blendable Curves, by contrast, contain *both* concave and convex portions in *each* of the halves. But don't be daunted; these curves are actually easier to work with! No pinning is necessary, and because the block is squared to size *after* the halves are sewn together, very little accuracy is required. You may never go back to traditional piecing after you experience the freedom of Blendable Curves.

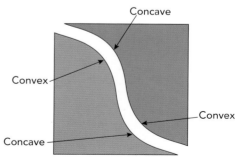

The Blendable Curve

The Blendable Curve technique has two variations: the free-form curve is either cut through pieced blocks or through squares of unpieced fabric. The variation you choose depends on which traditional quilt block you select.

BLOCKS WITH SQUARES AND RECTANGLES ONLY

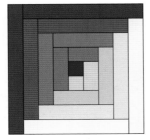

Traditional Nine Patch and Log Cabin blocks

Many beautiful traditional blocks are made up of only squares and rectangles. Two of my favorites are the Nine Patch and Log Cabin blocks. The Nine Patch block is made up of three rows of three squares, and the Log Cabin block is made up of rectangles surrounding a center square.

If you have chosen traditional blocks with squares and/or rectangles for your quilt, piece sets of blocks using a different color variation for each set. Follow the steps below to apply the curve to a stacked pair of completed blocks. Shuffling the halves of the cut blocks will give you new, abstract blocks that are a combination of your original color variations.

1. STACK. Layer 2 completed quilt blocks together **right sides up**. The abstract nature of this technique means you don't need to worry about exact alignment of the seams; just roughly align the top, bottom and side edges of the 2 blocks.

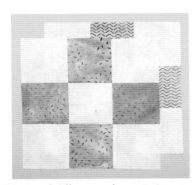

Stack blocks of different color variations together.
(Align edges before cutting.)

2. SLICE. With a sharp rotary cutter, cut a free-form curve diagonally from corner to corner, coming right in and right off at the points. Try to avoid cutting through any seam intersections, unless you feel comfortable with bulk in the seam allowance of your curve. Your cut should create a gentle curve that contains both concave and convex portions.

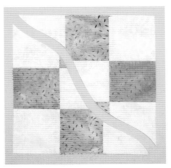

Notice how the Blendable Curve is cut to avoid seam intersections.

3. SHUFFLE. Once you have cut the curve, move 1 half of the top block to the corresponding bottom position. Now the top left and right halves will make a new block, and the bottom left and right halves will make a new block. Note that every time you cut a free-form curve through a pair of blocks, the resulting half-blocks are uniquely fitted to each other and are not interchangeable with other half-blocks.

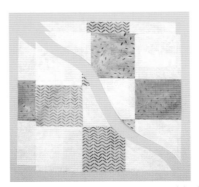

Shuffling block halves creates 2 new blocks with Blendable Curves.

4. SEW. You can sew these new blocks together as you go, or you can pin the correct halves together and set them aside to sew later.

If, after you've sewn the two halves together, the block is excessively warped and won't lie flat, check to make sure that you haven't sewn two right or two left sides together.

If you are uncomfortable with cutting a free-form curve, you can use one of the templates provided on page 61. You will quickly feel at ease going free-form, I promise; but for some projects, using a template actually provides you with *more* design opportunities. Curves cut with templates are identical in shape and thus interchangeable across all your color variations, as long as you keep left and right sides in their proper orientation.

BLOCKS WITH POINTS

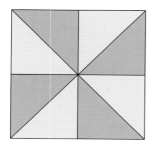

Traditional Pinwheel and Sawtooth Star blocks

Many traditional quilt blocks, such as the Pinwheel or Sawtooth Star blocks, contain the tips or "points" of triangles. For these types of blocks, the Blendable Curve technique is used to create the half- or quarter-square triangle units that contain these points. Rather than piecing blocks and cutting the curve through them, you cut the curve through squares of solid fabric.

If you have chosen these types of blocks for your quilt, cut solid squares in two colors and stack a pair together **right sides up**. Use a sharp rotary cutter to cut your free-form Blendable Curve from corner to opposite corner and move one half of the top block to the corresponding bottom position. This shuffling will give you two new half-square triangle blocks that are a combination of your original two colors.

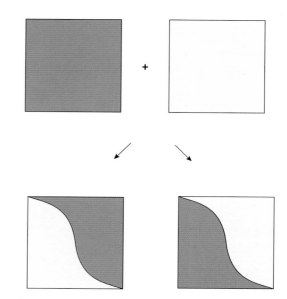

Use the new blocks on their own or piece them together with solid squares to make blocks with points, such as the Sawtooth Star.

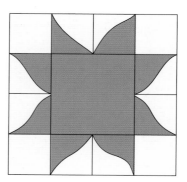

Or, try stacking two half-square triangle blocks and cutting an additional Blendable Curve to make quarter-square triangle blocks.

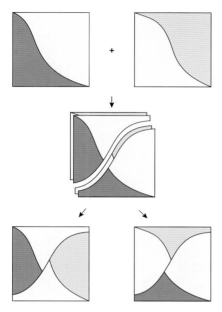

Use the quarter-square triangle blocks to make Blendable Curve Pinwheels or whatever other blocks you can think of.

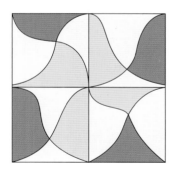

PRESSING

Good pressing habits are a huge factor in the success of a quilt. Most people recommend always pressing seams toward darker fabrics so that the seam allowance doesn't show through light-colored fabrics. However, I believe your *first* consideration should be the proper nesting of seams when the blocks are joined together into a quilt top.

When and How to Press?

I recommend pressing each time you sew a seam. Decide which fabric the seam allowance will be pressed toward and place that fabric face up. First press the seam to set the stitches. Then use your fingers to part the fabrics and gently press the edge of the iron against the bulk of the seam to fully expose the fabric. Press only from the front side of the fabric so that you can see whether the seam is opening to its fullest. Too often I see quilts that have a small fold at the seamline. This fold consumes valuable block size and will affect how the seams and blocks come together when you assemble the quilt top.

Pressed Seams and Quilting

Another consideration for pressing direction is the finished quilting design. For instance, quilting in the ditch is done on the side of the seam without a seam allowance. Quilting on this side compresses the layers next to the bulk of the seam, helping to lift the area forward and make it more visually prominent. When the seam allowances switch sides at an intersection, you need to take a stitch or two to reach the appropriate side to continue quilting.

Steam or No Steam?

Another issue is the use of steam. I am not a proponent of the use of steam in *most cases*, though there are *always* exceptions to every rule. Steam causes the edges of cut fabric to swell, and as the fabric dries and cools, the cut edges warp slightly, distorting the block. If you cannot live without steam in your quilting life, then keep your free hand in your pocket when ironing, to avoid the habit of pulling and stretching the fabric.

SEWING THE CURVE

Because the block halves being sewn together are cut larger than the finished size and then squared perfectly to size, a high level of accuracy is not required. In addition, because this technique yields an abstract look and feel, the seam intersections of the two halves don't need to match perfectly, so you don't have to be afraid of sewing curves. Just follow the step-by-step directions and discover how easy sewing curves can be!

Because each block half contains *both* a concave and a convex curve, you can't simply bring the raw edges of the entire block together at once and sew a scant ¼″ seam as usual. Instead, prepare the raw edges to meet only a few stitches ahead of the needle by always manipulating the concave area, whether it presents itself on the top or the bottom half of the block.

1. To minimize block-size loss, place the 2 halves of your block right sides together and align the straight edges and the corners.

2. Pivot the top half-block to bring the curved raw edges together at the tip of the block.

3. Place the very tip of the stack under the needle and take a few stitches to anchor the halves together. If your machine has a needle-down setting, engage it. The needle will act as a third finger holding the fabric in place when the presser foot is raised, so you can align the raw edges more easily. The needle will also prevent the 2 halves from slipping and shifting away from each other.

4. Bend the concave edge to meet the convex edge and press your finger at the edge of the concave area to create slight tension as you continue to bend and wrap the area to meet the convex curve. Be careful not to overstretch the fabric's edge. Stop sewing with your needle down whenever you need to realign the 2 halves of your block.

SQUARING UP

Creating the blocks larger than their final size allows you to relax and enjoy the cutting and piecing process because a high level of accuracy is not required for the block's final appearance. The final block size is determined by the size of your smallest block, so sometimes your finished quilt will be just a little smaller than you originally planned. No big deal. Remember—only lemonade at this stand.

Identify your smallest block and use a 12½˝ square ruler to determine the largest size it will square to. Let's say your smallest block will square to 5˝ × 5˝. Center the block within the square created by the 5˝ lines on the ruler. Align the 45° line of the ruler as close as possible with the sewn curved seam. The upper and lower points of the curved seam should be directly on the 45° line. This will ensure that when the block is sewn in next to its neighbors, you will have the sharpest point possible in the design. However, if you want to emphasize the abstract nature of the design, feel free to place the ruler on the block, trim the excess fabric from just two sides, turn the block, and repeat. You will now need to square the rest of your blocks to 5˝ × 5˝.

Note the design difference between a traditional star block and a Blendable Curve star block. You are making a traditional block uniquely your own.

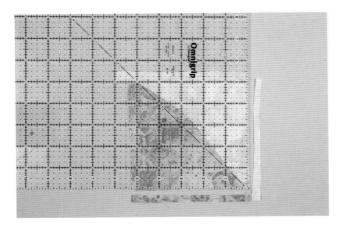

Your blocks are ready to be incorporated into your design. Now the fun really begins!

blended nines

2005, Peggy J. Barkle

Finished block size 4¼″ × 4¼″   Finished quilt size 35½″ × 44″   Quilt set 6 × 8

FABRIC REQUIREMENTS

Fabric amounts are based on a 42″ fabric width and strips cut from selvage to selvage on the crosswise grain, unless otherwise noted.

- ⅓ yard yellow fabric
- ⅓ yard orange fabric
- ⅓ yard light blue fabric
- ⅓ yard green fabric

- ½ yard light multicolored fabric
- ½ yard purple fabric
- ¼ yard inner-border fabric*
- ¾ yard outer-border fabric*

  * *Border yardage based on butted borders, sides sewn on first.*

- ⅝ yard bias-binding fabric for 2½″-wide double-fold binding
- 1⅝ yards backing fabric
- 42″ × 50″ batting

CUTTING AND PIECING INSTRUCTIONS FOR A NINE PATCH BLOCK

Refer back to this section when you need a refresher on constructing a Nine Patch block.

Cut all strips from selvage to selvage.

1. From both the yellow and the orange fabrics, cut 3 strips 2¼″ wide (6 strips total).

2. From both the light blue and the green fabrics, cut 3 strips 2¼″ wide (6 strips total).

3. From both the light multicolored and purple fabrics, cut 6 strips 2¼″ wide (12 strips total).

4. Sew 1 yellow strip and 2 orange strips together along their long edges into an orange/yellow/orange strip unit (A). Sew 1 orange strip and 2 yellow strips into a yellow/orange/yellow strip unit (B). Press the seams open.

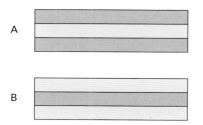

5. Repeat Step 4 with the light blue and green strips to create 1 A and 1 B strip unit.

6. Repeat Step 4 with the light multicolored and purple strips to create 2 A and 2 B strip units.

7. Subcut 18 segments 2¼″ wide from each strip unit and set the segments aside in separate piles. These segments will be used to create the Nine Patch blocks.

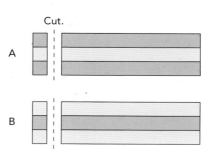

BLOCK CONSTRUCTION

The Nine Patch block is made up of 3 rows of 3 squares created by sewing together the segments subcut from the strip units. Half of the blocks should be constructed with the lighter fabric on the corners, and half should be constructed with the darker fabric on the corners. This alternation prevents identical fabrics from butting up against each other when the quilt top is assembled. Press the seams open.

A B A

B A B

Notice the difference in the corners of the 2 Nine Patches. The block with dark corners is made with A/B/A segments and the block with light corners is made with B/A/B segments.

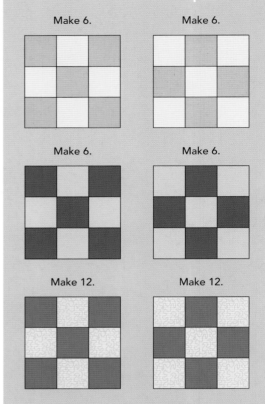

Make 6.   Make 6.

Make 6.   Make 6.

Make 12.   Make 12.

Blended Nines is one of four patterns in this book that use the traditional Nine Patch block. This is my favorite traditional block. It is easy to make, and application of the Blendable Curve technique to this block adds a lot of visual movement to a quilt's design.

CREATING THE BLENDABLE CURVE

Pair blocks with the opposite light/dark fabric placement. Blocks with dark corners should be paired with blocks with light corners. For step-by-step instructions on creating the Blendable Curve, see pages 5–11.

1. Pair the following blocks **right sides up** in sets of 2. Cut the Blendable Curve through the pairs and shuffle into new blocks.

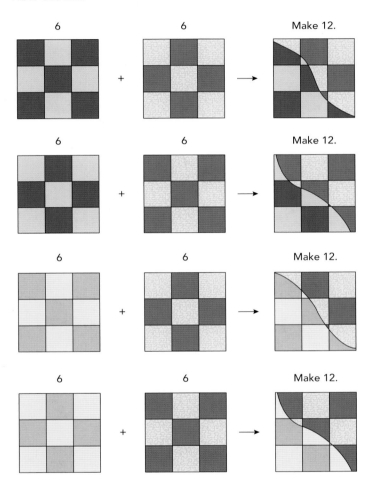

6   6   Make 12.

6   6   Make 12.

6   6   Make 12.

6   6   Make 12.

2. Sew the halves of the new blocks together and press the seams open. Square the blocks to 4¾˝ × 4¾˝ or to the size of your smallest block.

Creating the Blendable Curve: Stack, slice, shuffle, and sew.

ASSEMBLY

Use the assembly diagram to assemble the blocks into the quilt top and press well. Be mindful of how the blocks are oriented within the design. Apply a 1½˝ cut-width inner border and a 4½˝ cut-width outer border using your favorite border application method.

Assembly diagram

NOTES ON QUILTING

The quilting motifs should not interrupt the strong blended appearance of the design, and the thread color shouldn't compete with the colors of the quilt. Because the border of my quilt had a botanical feel and the predominant color was turquoise, I chose a flowing fern design in a turquoise thread.

Zingaro quilting motif, copyright © 2005 by Sue Patten of Golden Threads

See No-Fail Mitered Bindings (page 58) for directions on how to apply your binding.

the cat's napping in
the queen's garden

2006, Peggy J. Barkle

Finished block size 8″ × 8″   Finished quilt size 46″ × 62″   Quilt set 4 × 6

3. Cut out the traced shape and then cut away the center of the fusible web, except for approximately ¼″ to the inside line of your design. Fuse the "window pane" to the back of the flower.

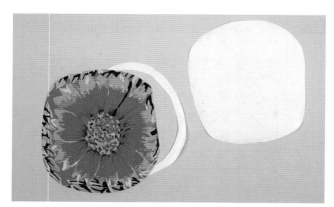

An example of window paning. Notice that the center has been cut away, leaving approximately ¼″ around the edge.

4. Repeat Steps 1–3 with enough flowers to cover all the intersections of the framing strips.

5. Freehand draw leaves to go with your flowers. Cut as many or as few leaves as you desire.

6. At this point you may choose to fuse the appliqués to the intersections of the framing strips and incorporate them into the final quilting design, or you can wait until the piece is quilted before adding them. I completed my quilting first. Because the quilting design I chose was rather dense, I did not want any quilting on top of the appliqués. However, leaving this area unquilted would have created a distortion in my finished quilt. So, I quilted first and appliquéd second.

7. Secure the edges of the fused appliqués with a ladder or zigzag stitch in matching thread.

NOTES ON QUILTING

Using a thread color that blended with the quilt's interior, I chose a freehand design to mimic the appliqué flowers. Petal shapes are stitched in the space created between the seams of each curve. The matching thread color creates a textural backdrop to the stunning appliqué flowers.

Petal quilting motif by Peggy J. Barkle

See No-Fail Mitered Bindings (page 58) for directions on how to apply your binding.

which road leads home?

2006, Peggy J. Barkle

Finished block size $6\frac{1}{2}'' \times 6\frac{1}{2}''$ Finished quilt size $45\frac{1}{2}'' \times 58\frac{1}{2}''$ Quilt set 7×9

FABRIC REQUIREMENTS

Fabric amounts are based on a 42″ fabric width and strips cut from selvage to selvage on the crosswise grain, unless otherwise noted.

- ⅝ yard yellow center-square fabric

- ⅓ yard each of 8 blue fabrics

- ⅓ yard each of 8 purple fabrics

- ¾ yard bias-binding fabric for 2½″-wide double-fold binding

- 3¾ yards backing fabric (seam to run the length of grain)

- 52″ × 65″ batting

CUTTING AND PIECING INSTRUCTIONS

Refer to page 13 for a refresher on Nine Patch piecing.

Cut all strips from selvage to selvage.

1. From the yellow center-square fabric, cut 6 strips 3″ wide.

2. From each of the 8 blue fabrics, cut 3 strips 3″ wide (24 strips total).

3. From each of the 8 purple fabrics, cut 3 strips 3″ wide (24 strips total).

4. Make 3 strip units of various combinations of blue/yellow/blue. Press the seams open. Subcut 32 segments 3″ wide from the strip units.

5. Make 3 strip units of various combinations of purple/yellow/purple. Press the seams open. Subcut 32 segments 3″ wide from the strip units.

6. Make 6 strip units of various combinations of 3 blue fabrics. Press the seams open. Subcut 64 segments 3″ wide from the strip units.

7. Make 6 strip units of various combinations of 3 purple fabrics. Press the seams open. Subcut 64 segments 3″ wide from the strip units.

BLOCK CONSTRUCTION

Because you are using 8 different fabrics of each color for this quilt, you don't have to make half of the Nine Patch blocks with light corners and half with dark. Only the center fabric must be set in a specific place; the placement of the other fabrics and the pairing of the blocks after you cut the curve will be up to you. Feel free to mix the placement of the fabrics in the blocks.

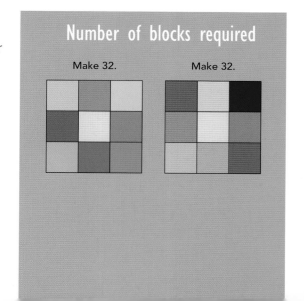

Number of blocks required

Make 32.   Make 32.

CREATING THE BLENDABLE CURVE

For step-by-step instructions on creating the Blendable Curve, see pages 5–11.

1. Pair blue and purple blocks **right sides up** in sets of 2. Cut the Blendable Curve through the pairs and shuffle into new blocks.

2. Sew the halves of the new blocks together and press the seams open. Square the blocks to 7″ × 7″ or to the size of your smallest block. You will have 64 blocks. One block will be left over after assembling your quilt top.

Creating the Blendable Curve: Stack, slice, shuffle, and sew.

ASSEMBLY

Use the assembly diagram to assemble the blocks into the quilt top and press well. This quilt has no borders.

Assembly diagram

NOTES ON QUILTING

Because the design of this quilt is so graphic, any highly stylized quilting won't be appreciated visually. I used a turquoise thread to blend with the background and Jodi Beamish's *Wild at Heart* design for the quilting motif.

Wild at Heart quilting motif, copyright © 2005 by Jodi Beamish of Willow Leaf Studio Designs

See No-Fail Mitered Bindings (page 58) for directions on how to apply your binding.

This quilt is constructed from a shaded Nine Patch block that offers all the design possibilities of a Log Cabin block when set into a quilt but requires much less piecing. Rather than the two fabrics of a traditional Nine Patch, this quilt is made up of eight blue fabrics and eight purple fabrics with the same color center square in each block.

curvaceous cabins

2005, Peggy J. Barkle

Finished block size 11″ × 11″   Finished quilt size 66″ × 77″   Quilt set 6 × 7

FABRIC REQUIREMENTS

When choosing fabrics, think about the division the curve creates in the block. If you want the curve to be well defined, choose fabrics with a high contrast. If you want a softer transition, choose fabrics that have similar values. You will need 4 light fabrics and 4 dark fabrics as well as a center-square fabric.

Fabric amounts are based on a 42˝ fabric width and strips cut from selvage to selvage on the crosswise grain, unless otherwise noted.

- ¾ yard light fabric #1
- 1 yard light fabric #2
- 1½ yards light fabric #3
- 1⅝ yards light fabric #4
- ¾ yard dark fabric #1

- 1 yard dark fabric #2
- 1½ yards dark fabric #3
- 1⅝ yards dark fabric #4
- ¼ yard center-square fabric

- ⅞ yard bias-binding fabric for 2½˝-wide double-fold binding
- 4¾ yards backing fabric (seam to run the length of grain)
- 72˝ × 83˝ batting

CUTTING AND PIECING INSTRUCTIONS FOR A LOG CABIN BLOCK

Refer back to this section when you need a refresher on constructing a Log Cabin block. I have altered the traditional piecing instructions for this block to compensate for the distortion that will be created in the cutting and sewing of the curve.

Cut all strips from selvage to selvage.

1. From both the light and the dark fabrics #1, cut 11 strips 2˝ wide (22 strips total).

2. From both the light and the dark fabrics #2, cut 15 strips 2˝ wide (30 strips total).

3. From both the light and the dark fabrics #3, cut 24 strips 2˝ wide (48 strips total).

4. From both the light and the dark fabrics #4, cut 27 strips 2˝ wide (54 strips total).

5. Label these strips with their fabric numbers (#1, #2, #3, #4). These labels will help you determine the positions of the strips in the Log Cabin block.

6. From the center-square fabric, cut 2 strips 2˝ wide.

BLOCK CONSTRUCTION

The Log Cabin block is created from rectangular strips pieced around a center square and is *traditionally* constructed so that one side of the block is made from dark strips and the other from light strips. In this project, however, you will create entirely dark blocks and entirely light blocks, and the half dark/half light effect will be achieved via the Blendable Curve.

1. With right sides together, sew a strip of center-square fabric to 1 strip of dark fabric #1 and press the seam away from the center-square fabric. Subcut the strip into 21 segments 2″ wide.

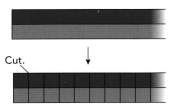

Cut.

2. With rights sides together, chain piece the 21 units from Step 1 to strips of dark fabric #1 (join the subcuts along their longer side to the strips of dark fabric #1). Press the seams open. Subcut the strips into 21 segments.

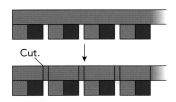

Cut.

3. Continue counterclockwise to add and subcut until the center square has been surrounded by fabric #1. Always press the seam open.

The beautiful curved lines that the Blendable Curves technique brings to the traditional Log Cabin block are stunning. This mix of traditional and contemporary has become a favorite of mine, and I hope it will become one of yours, too. There are so many setting options, and each gives a distinct look. Try turning the blocks in various directions to see what design possibilities exist.

Number of blocks required

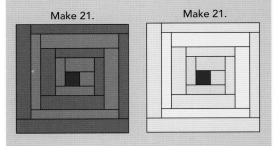

Make 21.　　　Make 21.

4. The blocks should measure 5″ × 5″ at this point. Use a 12½″ ruler to resize the blocks to 4½″ × 4½″ by trimming only the 2 sides with the longest strips (C and D).

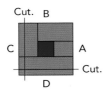

5. Repeat Steps 2–3 with fabric #2. Start by joining the blocks along side A to the strip of fabric #2. Square the blocks to 7″ × 7″ by trimming sides A and B, which are *opposite* the sides you trimmed last.

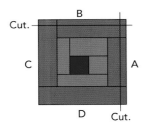

6. Repeat Steps 2–3 with fabric #3. Start by joining the blocks along side A to the strip of fabric #3. Square the blocks to 9½″ × 9½″ by trimming sides C and D, which are *opposite* the sides you trimmed last.

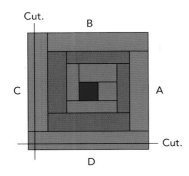

7. Repeat Steps 2–3 with fabric #4. Start by joining the blocks along side A to the strip of fabric #4. The blocks should measure 12½″ × 12½″. **Do not resize the blocks at this time.** You will have 21 dark blocks.

8. Construct the light-fabric blocks in the same manner described for the dark-fabric blocks. You will need 21 of them.

CREATING THE BLENDABLE CURVE

For step-by-step instructions on creating the Blendable Curve, see pages 5–11.

1. Pair half of the light blocks with half of the dark blocks **right sides up** in sets of 2, keeping the wide and skinny logs in the same orientation from one block to the next. Cut the Blendable Curve through the pairs and shuffle into new blocks. Remember that the abstract nature of this technique does not require you to match seam intersections.

2. Sew the halves of the new blocks together and press the seams open. Square the blocks to 11½″ × 11½″ by trimming the 2 sides *opposite* the sides you trimmed last. Squaring up the blocks after they have been cut and rejoined allows you to compensate for the distortion of the block created by the cutting and sewing process.

Creating the Blendable Curve: Stack, slice, shuffle, and sew.

ASSEMBLY

Use the assembly diagram to assemble the blocks into the quilt top and press well. Set the wider outside logs up against the thinner logs of the neighboring block to add visual interest to the final design. This quilt has no borders.

Assembly diagram

NOTES ON QUILTING

An allover quilting pattern is wonderful for this design. I used a pattern that incorporated both curves and points, but a pattern with soft curves or a rounded design will accentuate the curve of the pattern and be quite lovely. I matched the color of the thread closely to the color of the quilt so that the graphic design was not interrupted by the pattern or thread.

Free-form quilting motif by Peggy J. Barkle

See No-Fail Mitered Bindings (page 58) for directions on how to apply your binding.

pleasantville

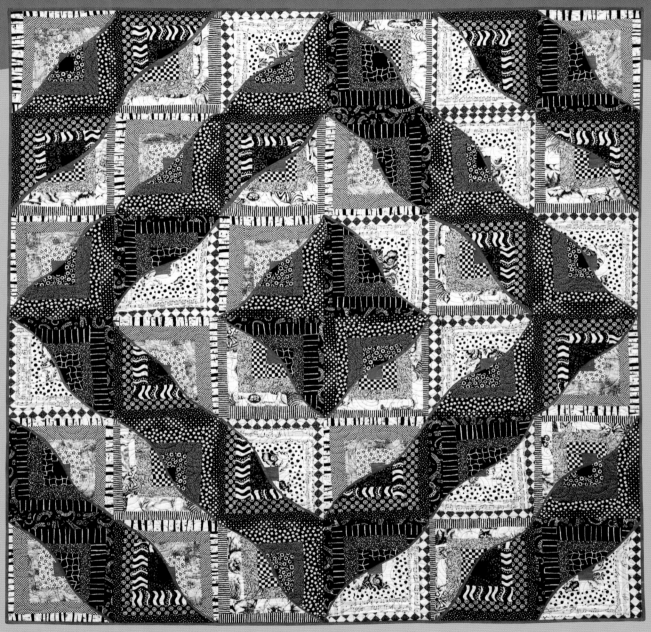

2006, Peggy J. Barkle

Finished block size 11″ × 11″   Finished quilt size 66″ × 66″   Quilt set 6 × 6

FABRIC REQUIREMENTS

Fabric amounts are based on a 42″ fabric width and strips cut from selvage to selvage on the crosswise grain, unless otherwise noted.

- ⅝ yard light fabric #1
- 1 yard light fabric #2
- 1¼ yards light fabric #3
- 1½ yards light fabric #4
- ⅝ yard dark fabric #1

- 1 yard dark fabric #2
- 1¼ yards dark fabric #3
- 1½ yards dark fabric #4
- 1 yard red fabric for center squares and bias accent strips

- ⅛ yard black fabric for center squares
- ⅞ yard bias-binding fabric for 2½″-wide double-fold binding
- 4⅛ yards backing fabric (seam to run the length of grain)
- 72″ × 72″ batting

This pattern is a variation of *Curvaceous Cabins* but with ¾″ bias strips pieced between the free-form curves. Piecing the bias strips into the curves requires that you handle the blocks and their exposed bias edges one more time than in the previous project, and this extra handling exposes the edges to more potential distortion.

In making this version, you must be willing to suffer more block-size loss and the uneven narrowing of strips that occurs at the outer edges of the completed blocks. If visual symmetry is important to you, don't use a fabric that has a defined linear design to it on the outside edge of the Log Cabin blocks; instead use a fabric with an allover design.

CREATING AND ADDING BIAS STRIPS TO THE BLENDABLE CURVE

When blocks contain curved edges, it is best to cut strips on the bias because they will stretch to accommodate the curves. To cut bias strips, align the straight edge of the fabric with the horizontal line of your cutting mat. Position your ruler so that the 45° mark is aligned with the straight edge of the fabric, and cut. For strips, move the ruler over the desired strip width and make another cut.

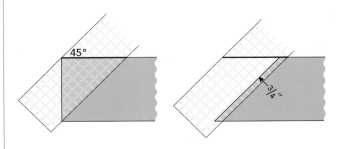

Align edge of fabric with 45° mark and cut.

Move ruler to desired width and cut.

CUTTING INSTRUCTIONS

These cutting instructions apply to both the light and dark fabrics.

Cut all strips from selvage to selvage.

1. From both the light and dark fabrics #1, cut 9 strips 2″ wide (18 strips total).

2. From both the light and dark fabrics #2, cut 14 strips 2″ wide (28 strips total).

3. From both the light and dark fabrics #3, cut 20 strips 2″ wide (40 strips total).

4. From both the light and dark fabrics #4, cut 23 strips 2″ wide (46 strips total).

5. Label these strips with their fabric number (#1, #2, #3, #4). These labels will help you determine the positions of the strips in the Log Cabin block.

6. From the red and black center-square fabrics, cut 1 strip 2″ wide (2 strips total).

7. From the red bias accent fabric, cut 2 strips 14″ wide. Subcut into 34 bias strips ¾″ wide.

BLOCK CONSTRUCTION

The Log Cabin block is created from rectangular strips pieced around a center square and is *traditionally* constructed so that one side of the block is made from dark strips and the other from light strips. In this project, however, you will create entirely dark blocks and entirely light blocks, and the half dark/half light effect will be achieved via the Blendable Curve.

INSTRUCTIONS

For step-by-step instructions on creating the Blendable Curve, see pages 5–11.

1. Complete all the Log Cabin blocks. The block construction instructions are the same as those in *Curvaceous Cabins* (page 28) except that you are creating 18 dark and 18 light blocks instead of 21.

Note: The white blocks are made with a red center square as in the previous project and the black blocks use a black center square.

2. Pair the light and dark blocks **right sides up** in sets of 2, keeping the logs in the same orientation from one block to the next. Cut the Blendable Curve through the pairs and shuffle into new blocks. Remember that the pairs are now uniquely fitted to each other, so you must keep track of the pairs when you add the bias strips.

3. Place a ¾″ bias strip right sides together with half of a cut block. The strip should extend at least ½″ beyond the block's edges. Anchor the strip with a few stitches and apply slight pressure to bend and shape the bias strip so it will conform to the raw edge of the curve. Sew using a scant ¼″ seam. (See page 10 for how to manipulate and sew curved edges.)

4. Align the curved edge of the other half of the block with the raw edge of the bias strip, right sides together. Sew with the bias strip on top, again manipulating the raw edge of the bias strip with slight pressure so it will meet and conform to the edge of the other half-block.

5. Press one seam toward the center and one away from the center. Make sure pleats are not pressed into the strip and that the entire seam is exposed.

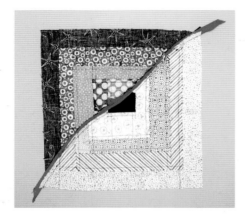

6. Repeat Steps 3–5 for the remaining blocks.

7. Using your 12½″ square ruler, square the blocks to 11½″ × 11½″ or to the size of your smallest block, trimming on the sides opposite the sides you trimmed last.

ASSEMBLY

Use the assembly diagram to assemble the blocks into the quilt top and press well. Set the wider outside logs up against the thinner logs of the neighboring block to add visual interest to the final design. This quilt has no borders.

Assembly diagram

NOTES ON QUILTING

As you can see from the photo on page 31, this quilt is quite graphic and busy. I'm not sure any thread choice or quilting option would really show. As a result I chose a red thread to complement the bias strip. I chose a circular pantograph (*Dizzy* by Jodi Beamish) to add texture and movement.

Dizzy quilting motif, copyright © 2005 by Jodi Beamish of Willow Leaf Studio Designs

See No-Fail Mitered Bindings (page 58) for directions on how to apply your binding.

curve-azy stars

2005, Peggy J. Barkle

FABRIC REQUIREMENTS

Fabric amounts are based on a 42″ fabric width and strips cut from selvage to selvage on the crosswise grain, unless otherwise noted.

- 1½ yards yellow fabric (For ease, instructions use only 1 yellow for the floating squares.)
- 1 fat quarter each of 30 different star fabrics
- 1⅝ yards background fabric
- ½ yard pink fabric
- ⅜ yard inner-border fabric*
- 2¼ yards outer-border fabric* (strips cut on lengthwise grain)
- ⅞ yard bias-binding fabric for 2½″-wide double-fold binding
- 5¼ yards backing fabric (seam to run the length of grain)
- 80″ × 92″ batting

* *Border yardage based on butted borders, sides sewn on first.*

I love the look of this quilt, particularly the floating squares that result when two stars lie next to each other. Another fun element is the pink butterfly unit formed where the tips of two half-square triangles touch. The quilt is visually striking because each star is made of a different fabric. No two stars are alike, just like in the night sky.

CUTTING INSTRUCTIONS

Cut all strips from selvage to selvage.

Note: This is the first project where the Blendable Curves are cut through squares of unpieced fabric rather than through pieced blocks.

Yellow Squares

From the yellow fabric, cut 11 strips 4½″ wide. Subcut the strips into 98 squares 4½″ × 4½″.

Star Squares

1. From each of the 30 star fabrics, cut 1 square 6½″ × 6½″ for the star centers.

2. From each of the 30 star fabrics, cut 4 squares 4½″ × 4½″ for the star points.

3. From the background fabric, cut 3 strips 4½″ wide. Subcut the strips into 22 squares 4½″ × 4½″ for the star points.

4. From the background fabric, cut 7 strips 3½″ wide. Subcut the strips into 80 squares 3½″ × 3½″ for the star block corners.

Pink Butterfly Corners

1. From the pink butterfly fabric, cut 3 strips 4½″ wide. Subcut the strips into 20 squares 4½″ × 4½″.

2. From the background fabric, cut 3 strips 4½″ wide. Subcut the strips into 20 squares 4½″ × 4½″.

BLOCK CONSTRUCTION

The trick to this quilt is keeping track of all the elements. Notice in the photo (page 35) for instance, that the interior star points are paired with a different fabric than the perimeter star points. For this quilt, having a large working space or a design board really helps. Lay out your pieces as you go, referring to the assembly diagram (page 38).

CREATING THE BLENDABLE CURVE

For step-by-step instructions on creating the Blendable Curve, see pages 5–11.

Pink Butterfly Corners

Pair the 20 pink squares 4½″ × 4½″ with 20 background-fabric squares **right sides up** in sets of 2. Stack, slice, shuffle, and sew. You will have 40 star corners. Press toward the pink fabric. Square the blocks to 3½″ × 3½″.

Make 40.

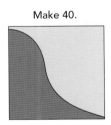

Corner Star Blocks

1. Select 4 matching star fabric squares, 4½″ × 4½″. Pair 2 of these with 2 yellow squares **right sides up** in sets of 2. Stack, slice, shuffle, and sew. You will have 4 star points. Press toward the star fabric. Square the blocks to 3½″ × 3½″.

2. Pair the other 2 matching star fabric squares 4½″ × 4½″ with 2 background-fabric squares **right sides up** in sets of 2.

Stack, slice, shuffle, and sew. You will have 4 star points. Press toward the star fabric. Square the blocks to 3½″ × 3½″.

3. Repeat Steps 1 and 2 to make 3 more sets of 8 matching star points.

4. Assemble the corner star blocks as illustrated below, using 1 matching star square 6½″ × 6½″ in the center and the star points prepared above. Two of the corner star blocks will have a pink butterfly block in 1 of their corners, and 2 will have all background fabric corners.

Make 2.

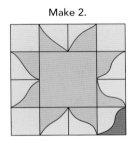

Make 2.

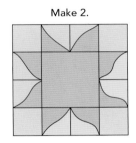

Perimeter Star Blocks

1. Select 4 matching star fabric squares, 4½″ × 4½″. Pair 3 of these with 3 yellow squares **right sides up** in sets of 2. Stack, slice, shuffle, and sew. You will have 6 star points. Press toward the star fabric. Square the blocks to 3½″ × 3½″.

2. Pair the 1 remaining star square with 1 background-fabric square **right sides up.** Stack, slice, shuffle, and sew. You will have 2 star points. Press toward the star fabric. Square the blocks to 3½″ × 3½″.

3. Repeat Steps 1 and 2 to make 13 more sets of 8 matching star points.

4. Assemble the perimeter star blocks as illustrated on page 38, using 1 matching star square 6½″ × 6½″ in the center and the star points prepared above. Press toward the star fabric. Seven of the perimeter star blocks will have pink butterfly blocks in 2 of the corner positions and 7 will have all background fabric corners.

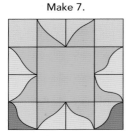

Make 7.

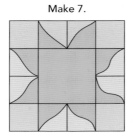

Make 7.

Interior Star Blocks

1. Select 4 matching star fabric squares, 4½″ × 4½″. Pair these with 4 yellow squares **right sides up** in sets of 2. Stack, slice, shuffle, and sew. You will have 8 star points. Press toward the star fabric. Square the blocks to 3½″ × 3½″.

2. Repeat Step 1 to make 11 more sets of 8 matching star points.

3. Assemble the interior star blocks as illustrated below, using 1 matching star square 6½″ × 6½″ in the center and the star points prepared above. Press toward the star fabric. Six of the interior star blocks will have pink butterfly blocks in each corner and 6 will have all background fabric corners.

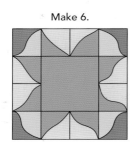

Make 6.

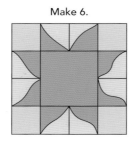

Make 6.

ASSEMBLY

Use the assembly diagram to assemble the blocks into the quilt top and press well. Keep in mind that the colors of the stars in the diagram may not match yours, depending on the 30 star fabrics you choose. Apply a 1½″ cut-width inner border and a 6½″ cut-width outer border using your favorite border application method.

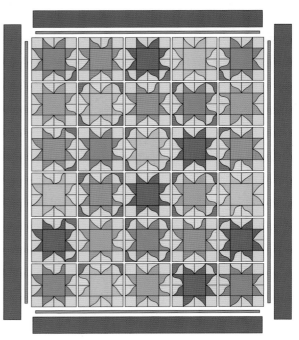

Assembly diagram

NOTES ON QUILTING

I chose another soft-edged allover pantograph pattern because I felt that a stylized quilting design would not enhance the quilt's finished look. I wanted the thread to have some impact on the quilt, so I chose a lime green thread to show up in the darker stars.

Splash quilting motif, copyright © 2004 by Jodi Beamish of Willow Leaf Studio Designs

See No-Fail Mitered Bindings (page 58) for directions on how to apply your binding.

art for four

2005, Peggy J. Barkle

Finished block size 4″ × 4″   **Finished quilt size** 30″ × 30″ *   **Quilt set** 6 × 6

* Finished quilt size will vary depending on the width of the curves cut into the borders.

CURVED BORDERS

You have to consider several factors when curving the borders of a quilt. How deeply you cut the curve to the left and right will affect the initial width of the border strip you start with. The cut border needs to include the approximate finished width plus seam allowance and, at a minimum, a 2″ to 3″ tolerance for the curve. Once you have layered the borders, you can cut the curve only within the area where the 2 borders overlap.

1. Place an inner border strip on a flat cutting surface **right side up**. Place a middle border strip **right side up** (matching centers) along one edge of the inner border, overlapping both lengthwise by 2″. Cut a soft, gentle curve through both the inner border and the middle border, being careful to stay within the 2″ overlap. Once you start the cut, anchor the pieces with a heavy object to avoid shifting of the fabric.

Borders overlap (match centers before cutting).

2. Remove the waste of the inner and middle borders from within the overlap. With tailor's chalk, apply hash marks across both borders. These hash marks are your roadmap to pinning and sewing your borders.

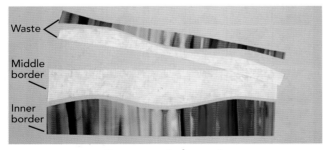

Remove waste from cut.

3. Pin the middle border to the inner border right sides together, matching the hash marks, and sew using a ¼″ seam. Press the seams away from the middle border. If the curve was cut too deeply, you may have to cut a clip in the seam allowance to help release the tension of the curve.

4. Repeat Steps 1–3 for the remaining 3 inner and middle border strips.

5. Repeat Steps 1–4 using the sewn inner/middle border from Step 3 and the outer border. Overlap the *straight* long edge of the middle border with a long edge of the outer border.

6. Use your favorite border application method to sew on the borders and miter the corners.

NOTES ON QUILTING

The quilting is a free-form spiral, accentuating the curve. A bright, variegated thread was used to create a textural surface on the background fabric.

A free-form spiral quilting motif by Peggy J. Barkle

See No-Fail Mitered Bindings (page 58) for directions on how to apply your binding.

pinwheel party

2005, Peggy J. Barkle

Finished block size 4″ × 4″   Finished Pinwheel block size 8″ × 8″

Finished quilt size 34″ × 42″   Quilt set 3 × 4

ASSEMBLY

Use the assembly diagram to assemble the blocks into the quilt top and press well. Apply a 1½˝ cut-width inner border and a 4½˝ cut-width outer border using your favorite border application method to sew on borders and miter the corners. (You will cut the curve in the outer edge of the outer border later, after quilting.)

Assembly diagram

Free-form quilting motif by Peggy J. Barkle

NOTES ON QUILTING

I used a free-form design that has soft curves and sharp points to mimic the shapes within the quilt. I didn't feel the colors in the quilt were strong enough to carry a dominant thread color, so I chose a soft, blended thread.

CURVED OUTER EDGE

After the piece has been quilted, cut a soft, gradual curve on the outside edge of the outer border to add interest and whimsy to the finished quilt. Anytime you want to cut and shape the outside edge of the outer border, you must first quilt your quilt. The cutting of the border releases the bias grain, which can stretch during the quilting process.

Place your quilt on a flat surface. Decide whether you want to round off the corners or create pointed corners as I did. Cut a free-form curve just slightly inside the border's edge. If you are more comfortable using a template, you can create one using freezer paper. Be sure to use bias binding so the binding will conform to the cut curves.

blown away

2005, Peggy J. Barkle

Finished block size 5″ × 5″   Finished Pinwheel block size 10″ × 10″

Finished quilt size 60″ × 70″   Quilt set 6 × 7

  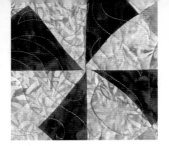 

FABRIC REQUIREMENTS

Fabric amounts are based on a 42″ fabric width and strips cut from selvage to selvage on the crosswise grain, unless otherwise noted.

- 4 yards blue fabric
- 3⅛ yards cream fabric
- ⅞ yard orange fabric
- ⅞ yard bias-binding fabric for 2½″-wide double-fold binding
- 4⅜ yards backing fabric (seam to run the length of grain)
- 66″ × 76″ batting

This variation on the Pinwheel pattern has a more sophisticated look. It is a great quilt for someone who likes dark colors and rich hues. The blocks in the interior are made predominantly of light background fabric, and the surrounding areas are made predominantly of dark fabric. The resulting positive/negative contrast is interesting. The high contrast between the outer blocks and the background of the interior blocks creates a wonderful hard edge up against the soft lines of the free-form curve.

CUTTING INSTRUCTIONS

Remember that for every free-form curve cut during a block's construction, 1″ extra is added to both the length and the width of the desired final block size, including the seam allowance. Because 2 curves will be cut in these blocks, I have added 2″ extra. If your seam allowance tolerances do not require as much, adjust the cut size of your squares accordingly.

Cut all strips from selvage to selvage.

1. From the blue fabric, cut 18 strips 7½″ wide. Subcut the strips into 86 squares 7½″ × 7½″.

2. From the cream fabric, cut 14 strips 7½″ wide. Subcut the strips into 70 squares 7½″ × 7½″.

3. From the orange fabric, cut 3 strips 7½″ wide. Subcut the strips into 12 squares 7½″ × 7½″.

CREATING THE BLENDABLE CURVE

For step-by-step instructions on creating the Blendable Curve, see pages 5–11.

Half-Square Triangle Blocks

1. Pair 42 blue squares with 42 cream squares **right sides up** in sets of 2. Cut the Blendable

Curve through the pairs and shuffle into new blocks.

2. Pair 12 orange squares with 12 cream squares **right sides up** in sets of 2. Cut the Blendable Curve through the pairs and shuffle into new blocks.

3. Sew the halves of the new blocks together and press the seams toward the darker fabrics. **Don't resize your blocks at this time**. You will have 84 blue/cream half-square triangle blocks and 24 orange/cream half-square triangle blocks.

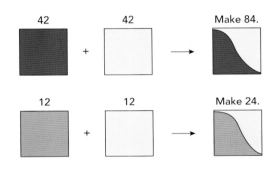

Outer Quarter-Square Triangle Blocks

Pair 44 blue/cream half-square triangle blocks with 44 blue squares **right sides up** in sets of 2. Cut a free-form curve along the diagonal opposite the first curve and shuffle and sew into new blocks. Press the seams open. Square the blocks to 5½˝ × 5½˝ or to the size of your smallest block. You will have 88 outer blocks.

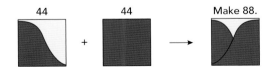

Interior Quarter-Square Triangle Blocks

Pair 16 blue/cream half-square triangle blocks with 16 cream squares **right sides up** in sets of 2. Cut a free-form curve along the diagonal opposite the first curve and shuffle and sew into new blocks. Press the seams open. Square the blocks to 5½˝ × 5½˝ or to the size of your smallest block. You will have 32 interior blocks.

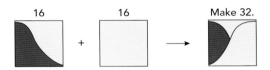

Blue and Orange Interior Quarter-Square Triangle Blocks

Pair 24 blue/cream half-square triangle blocks with 24 orange/cream half-square triangle blocks **right sides up** in sets of 2. Position the blocks so that the seams lie on top of one another and the blue and yellow fabrics are on *opposite* sides. Cut a free-form curve along the diagonal opposite the first curve and shuffle and sew into new blocks. Press the seams open. Square the blocks to 5½˝ × 5½˝ or to the size of your smallest block. You will have 48 blue/orange/cream quarter-square triangle interior blocks.

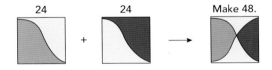

See *Art for Four* (page 41) for photo examples of creating quarter-square triangle blocks with Blendable Curves.

If you match the center seams when sewing the quarter-square triangles, you'll get a nice sharp point. Or, throw caution to the wind and allow the abstract nature of the design to show through by letting the points fall where they may.

ASSEMBLY

Use the assembly diagram to assemble the blocks into the quilt top and press well. This quilt has no borders.

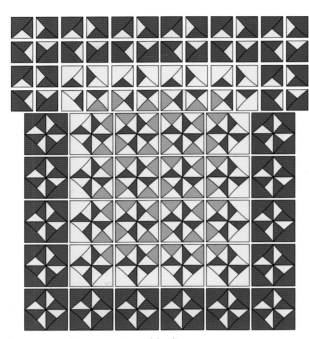

Assembly diagram

NOTES

The quilt's d⬚
strong. I felt
quilting desi⬚
the quilting ⬚
for a thread ⬚
and a leaf pa⬚
one of the fa⬚

Java quilting motif, copyright © 2005 by Sue Patten of Golden Threads

See No-Fail Mitered Bindings (page 58) for directions on how to apply your binding.

a leap of faith

2004, Peggy J. Barkle

Finished block size 8″ × 8″   **Finished quilt size** 58″ × 74″   **Quilt set** 6 × 8

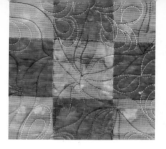   

Now that you've experimented with the Blendable Curve technique and feel comfortable with it, it's time to take *A Leap of Faith* and color outside the lines.

This is one of my favorite quilts and the springboard from which my Blendable Curve technique arose. I had wanted to design an artsy-type quilt because such quilts seemed to incorporate so many different elements and techniques, but I had no art training and no degree in textiles. I was a self-taught quilter and had no idea where or how to begin. How did these talented quilters come up with their ideas for those beautiful artsy quilts? I felt secure in my piecing abilities, but I was daunted by the vastness of the design possibilities.

Curved piecing was popular and something I had not really tried. What if I incorporated it into my favorite block, the Nine Patch? And thus it all began. I pulled several batiks (oh, to have a stash) in groups of two to make my Nine Patches and began sewing, slicing, and shuffling. When the blocks went up on the design wall, I was thrilled with the abstract look they were creating. Adding a plain, uncurved Nine Patch here and there changed the design on a dime.

Then I had a lightbulb moment. Perhaps some of those talented quilters had art degrees and textile backgrounds, but they had something else I did not have until that very moment: they believed in themselves enough to go out on that limb and be proud of what they had designed. Blendable Curves gave me that same confidence, and that's why this pattern is called *A Leap of Faith*.

PICKING YOUR FABRIC INSPIRATION

Picking a fabric inspiration can be as simple as choosing your favorite colors; the colors of a beautiful place you've visited; the colors of a spring, summer, winter, or fall day; or the colors of the ocean floor in the Caribbean or a tropical rainforest. What about ground, grass, water, sky, sun, or flowers? This is your vision, and anything can live there.

You are picking materials to create 8 to 12 different Nine Patch blocks. Pick your fabrics in sets of 2, just as you would for the traditional block. You will want to blend the colors of some Nine Patches and contrast the colors of others. Value will be your most important tool; be sure to pick a variety of lights, mediums, and darks.

FABRIC REQUIREMENTS

Fabric amounts are based on a 42″ fabric width and strips cut from selvage to selvage on the crosswise grain, unless otherwise noted.

- ½ yard each of 8–12 fabrics for Nine Patch blocks (add ¼ yard of any of these fabrics that you want to incorporate into the collaged border)

- ¼ yard each of 2 petal fabrics

- ¼ yard each of 2 sunflower fabrics

- ¼ yard stalk fabric

- ⅛ yard each of 2 leaf fabrics

- ⅞ yard bias-binding fabric for 2½″-wide double-fold binding

- 3 yards of assorted border fabric*

  * *Border yardage will vary depending on your border "collage" assembly.*

- 4⅝ yards backing fabric (seam to run the length of grain)

- 64″ × 80″ batting

- 1 yard fusible web or 22″ × 40″ batting (optional)

CUTTING INSTRUCTIONS

Refer to page 13 for a refresher on Nine Patch piecing.

Cut all strips from selvage to selvage.

From each of the 8–12 Nine Patch fabrics, cut strips 3½″ wide until you have a total of 21 strips of light fabric and 21 strips of dark fabric.

BLOCK CONSTRUCTION

1. Create strip units by combining light and dark fabrics (see page 13). Subcut each of the strip units into 12 segments 3½″ wide.

2. Select fabric groupings and construct 5–8 Nine Patch blocks from each.

CREATING THE BLENDABLE CURVE

For step-by-step instructions on creating the Blendable Curve, see pages 5–11.

1. Pair 4–5 of the Nine Patch blocks with 4–5 other Nine Patch blocks **right sides up** in sets of 2. If you have envisioned a spring meadow, think about pairing some green Nine Patches with purple and gold Nine Patches that could represent fields of flowers. Cut the Blendable Curve through the pairs and shuffle into new blocks.

2. Sew the halves of the new blocks together and press the seams open or to one side.

Creating the Blendable Curve: Stack, slice, shuffle, and sew.

3. Once you have made the first few blocks, play with them on a design wall and see what emerges. Create new designs by rotating the blocks. This process will give you ideas about what colors to combine in the remaining Nine Patches. Try incorporating an uncut Nine Patch block or mixing a plain square of fabric with 1 of your Blendable Curve cuts. By turning blocks in different directions, you can create winding paths of color, shape,

quick tips on quilting

My goal here is to give you some basic machine quilting tips to help you complete the projects in this book. Many wonderfully talented machine quilters and teachers have devoted entire books to this subject, but my aim is to get you started and maybe whet your appetite for machine quilting.

NEEDLE CHOICES

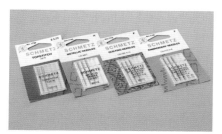

Machine quilting needles

For most quilting jobs, I use a machine quilting needle, size 90/14 or 75/11. I use a jeans needle if the quilt has been constructed from thicker fabrics because this needle has a sharp point and strong shaft. If you would like to quilt with a metallic thread, use a metallic 80/12 needle. The thread glides through the large eye with less friction and therefore less breakage occurs. You will, however, need to quilt at a slower pace when using metallic thread. A 100/16 topstitching needle is a good choice for bulkier threads because of its large eye.

THREAD CHOICES

Thread is no longer one-size-fits-all. Today thread comes in every color and every weight and can be made of cotton, rayon, metallic, polyester, or blends of all of these. The higher the thread weight, the thinner the thread. Pair a 12-weight thread with a 100/16 topstitching needle because of the larger eye, and pair a 60-weight thread with a 90/14 machine quilting needle because the thinner thread needs no special accommodation. Mettler 60-weight silk-finish cotton thread is a great place to start.

By all means experiment with all types of thread because each can add a wonderful look or spark to your work. Buying the best you can afford will ensure that the stitches in your quilt will last as long as your high-quality fabric.

BATTING CHOICES

There are many choices of batting on the market today for machine or hand quilting. They can be made of polyester, cotton, wool, silk, and even cashmere. There are also blends of all of these. The batting you choose is determined in part by what the quilt will be used for. Cotton breathes well, will be cooler than wool, and also has a lower loft.

Another consideration is quilting distances. Each batting has a quilting tolerance—that is, a minimum distance between lines of quilting—to secure the three layers together so that the batting will not shift over time. Get the very best for your project. Make sure you pick a machine-grade batting. Try them all and quilt a scrap of every batting you try, keeping notes on what you liked or disliked and why. A low-loft cotton batting is a great choice if are you just starting out. My recommendation if you're just starting out is *Warm and Natural* by The Warm

Company. It is an all-cotton batting with a quilting tolerance of 8″–10″. It will be easier to move and control. To figure the size of batting required for your project, add 6″ to both the finished length and the finished width of your quilt top because the batting will draw up as you quilt.

QUILTING WITH A WALKING FOOT

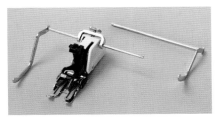

A quilter's walking foot and guide

A walking foot is an invaluable quilting tool. It works in combination with your sewing machine's feed dogs to feed the layers of your quilt evenly through the machine. Grid, crosshatch, stitch-in-the-ditch, and slightly curved quilting can all be performed with the aid of a walking foot. Many walking feet come with a guide that allows you to quilt evenly spaced lines by first marking a single line and then setting the guide to follow the first line at a specific quilting interval.

When you perform grid or crosshatch quilting, sewing the successive lines in opposite directions will prevent any

warping of the quilt. For slightly curved quilting, you will need to raise and lower your presser foot several times to follow the curve. If your machine has a needle-down setting, engage it. If not, remember to insert your needle into the quilt when pausing. This prevents the quilt from shifting when you begin quilting again. Increase the stitch length to accommodate the thickness of all three layers. There should be no visible signs of the fabric pulling or puckering on either side of the stitch.

FREE-MOTION QUILTING

Free-motion quilting feet

The feet for free-motion quilting can look very different from one another, although most will have a small spring behind the shaft of the foot. The two feet pictured perform the same job but allow a different level of control and give you a different view as you quilt. Free-motion quilting is achieved with your sewing machine's feed dogs either dropped or covered. Without the feed dogs, you control the

length of the stitches by how fast or slow you move the fabric with your hands in unison with the speed of your machine. Free-motion quilting truly is a practice-makes-perfect effort.

FREE-MOTION STITCH LENGTH

If your stitches are *too long*, you are running your machine *too slowly* and your fabric *too fast*. If your stitches are *too short*, you are running your machine *too fast* and your fabric *too slowly*. Also, the top tension may need to be adjusted to achieve a correct stitch. Continue to experiment with the tension until you find that sweet spot. Some older sewing machines were not made for the rigors of free-motion quilting. It can be quite hard on the machine's motor. If you have tried and tried to obtain the proper tension while free-motion quilting with these older "lovely ladies" and find yourself frustrated and annoyed, this may be the perfect time and reason to invest in a new machine.

PULLING UP YOUR BOBBIN THREAD

Whether you are quilting with a walking foot or a free-motion foot, here are some rules that apply to both. When you begin quilting, you will always need to pull your bobbin thread up through the layers of your quilt. Doing so will prevent an ugly thread nest from developing on the back. To do this, position your quilt under the needle where you will begin sewing. Hold onto the top thread, lower the presser foot, and hand cast the sewing machine wheel so that the needle penetrates all the layers of your quilt and then rises to its highest position again. Lift the presser foot and tug on the top thread; the bobbin thread should pop up to the top of the quilt. Using your finger or a pin, pull the bobbin

thread all the way out. Set the needle back in your quilt at the same spot, lower the presser foot, and be sure to take all the slack out of both threads.

KNOTTING OFF

Whenever you begin or end a line of quilting, you must secure the threads by knotting them off. There are several methods for doing this. Remember to pull up your bobbin thread first.

1. Holding your quilt to keep it from advancing, stitch in place 3 or 4 times.

2. Take a few stitches forward and then backward.

3. The most desirable and professional choice is burying your thread tails in the quilt. When you begin or end a line of quilting, make sure you leave long tails of the top and bobbin threads and make sure they are out of the way as you begin to quilt. Later, thread the tails onto a hand sewing needle, make a quilter's knot, and bury the threads in the batting, cutting away any excess.

Remember to practice, practice, and practice. And, above all, remember to have fun and always enjoy the journey.

no-fail mitered bindings

Whether you choose bias or straight-grain binding, the following instructions apply. Double-fold binding is often the choice for many quilters because of its strength and durability. Binding needs to be long enough to wrap all 4 sides of your quilt plus 10″ for turning corners and joining the ends. Strips of binding should be sewn together at a 45° angle, with the seams pressed open to reduce bulk.

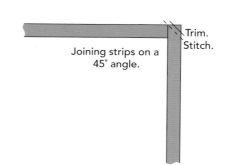

Joining strips on a 45° angle.

Trim.
Stitch.

1. Square your finished quilt. Place your prepared binding right sides together with the quilt top, with raw edges even, beginning in the middle of one side. Leave 10″ of beginning

binding unattached. Using a walking foot, begin sewing the binding to the quilt using a ¼″ seam.

2. Stop ¼″ away from the upcoming corner. Backstitch or sew off the corner at a 45° angle and remove the quilt from the machine. Fold the binding straight up so that the raw edge is aligned with the next edge of your quilt.

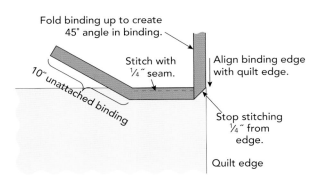

Fold binding up to create 45° angle in binding.

10″ unattached binding

Stitch with ¼″ seam.

Align binding edge with quilt edge.

Stop stitching ¼″ from edge.

Quilt edge

3. Fold the binding back on itself, raw edge even with the next edge of the quilt, making sure the fold created at the top edge of the binding is even with the top edge of the quilt. Place the quilt back under your machine and continue sewing. Continue this process until all 4 corners of the quilt are complete.

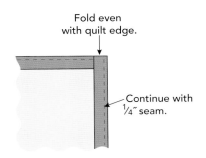

Fold even with quilt edge.

Continue with ¼″ seam.

4. Stop approximately 10″ from where you began stitching and backstitch. Remove the quilt from the machine and place it flat on your worktable.

5. Bring the 2 tails of the binding to the middle of the opening and overlap them; the amount of overlap depends on the width of the binding strips. If you used 2½″-wide binding, overlap the tails by 2½″; if you used 2¼″-wide binding, overlap the tails by 2¼″. Cut away the excess from both of the tails.

6. Open the right tail and flatten it right side up.

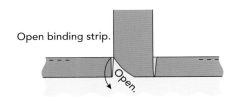

Open binding strip.

Open.

7. Open the left tail and place it right sides together with the right tail, creating an L.

8. Draw a diagonal line from the upper left corner to the lower right corner of the binding strip. Stitch on this line. Cut away the excess fabric to leave a ¼″ seam allowance and iron the seam open.

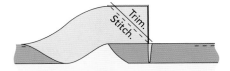

Trim.

Stitch.

9. Place the quilt flat again. The binding should fit perfectly. Slip the quilt back under your machine and finish sewing the binding to the quilt.

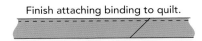

Finish attaching binding to quilt.

10. Roll the binding to the back of the quilt, and hand baste the folded edge to the quilt back with a slip stitch at least every ¼″.

If you choose to finish the binding by machine, apply the binding to the *back* of your quilt, following all the previous instructions. Roll the completed binding to the front of the quilt, so the folded edge sits right on top of the stitching line with which you applied the binding. Topstitch as close to the folded edge as possible.

> You can use a decorative stitch to secure the binding edge to the quilt front.

template patterns

Use freezer paper to create your templates. Press the shiny side to the material to give more stability when cutting.

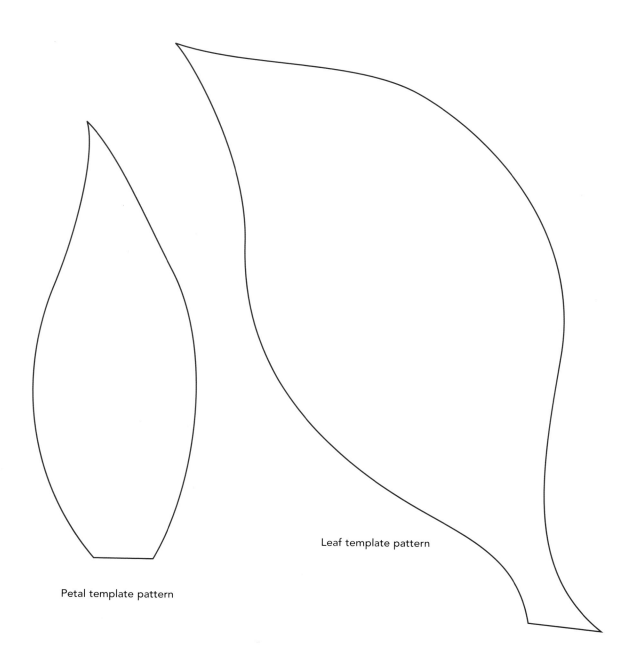

Petal template pattern

Leaf template pattern

If the size of your block is not represented here, use one of these two suggested curves and either extend or shorten it to meet your block requirements.

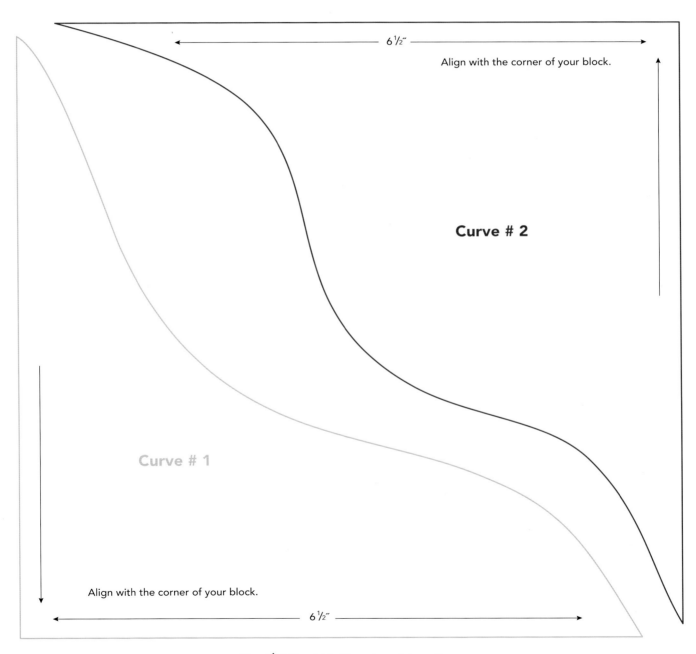

6½″

Align with the corner of your block.

Curve # 2

Curve # 1

Align with the corner of your block.

6½″

Two 6½″ Blendable Curve template patterns

gallery

Butterflies and Blooms, 53″ × 60″,
copyright © 2006 by Fay Rawls

JOY!, 58½″ × 71½″, copyright © 2006 by Sarah S. Hubbard

Priscilla's Plan,
23½″ × 39½″,
copyright © 2006 by
Priscilla Evans Hair

Bluebells, Cockle Shells, 57″ × 72″,
copyright © 2006 by Shirley Erickson

Sailing on the Wind, 31″ × 38″,
copyright © 2006 by Kristie J. Smith

Chaotic Order, 57″ × 73″,
copyright © 2006 by Lura J. Campbell

Time Flies, 31″ × 38″, copyright © 2006
by Donna Andersen

Purple Haze, 66″ × 72″,
copyright © 2006 by Mary M. Gibson

about the author

Peggy J. Barkle was born in Seattle, Washington, but grew up in the San Francisco Bay Area. She attended high school in San Francisco and studied interior design in college.

She met her husband, Ken, in 1979, and they were married in Carmel, California, in 1981. It was a beautiful place to start a life together and they doubled their pleasure when twins Ryan and Katie were born in 1984. Peggy decided to leave the corporate world to stay home and raise the children, but soon she was looking for relief from the endless bottles, diapers, and dishes that came along with being a young wife and mother.

She loved her kids more than anything and wouldn't have traded a minute with them, but at the end of the day, she needed to be able to look at and touch something that defined her as a person and not just as a wife a[...]
time she ran across a PBS seri[...]

hosted by Eleanor Burns, she had run through every craft known to man, but when she put fabric between her fingers, the search was over. She was hooked. She was home!

She began teaching in 1995 at a local quilt shop and area guilds. Her favorite students are the beginners, wide-eyed and eager. She has a room full of yardage and a brain full of ideas. She could not imagine doing anything else and considers being able to share what she loves an unbelievable blessing.

The family moved to Atlanta, Georgia, in 1995, after a brief stay in Arkansas. The kids are grown now, and fortunately so has Peggy's fabric stash.

[...] see Peggy's website:

RESOURCES

American & Efrid

Signature quilting thread and Mettler thread
P.O. Box 507
Mt. Holly, NC 28120
800-453-5128
www.amefird.com

Bernina USA

Sewing machines and accessories
3702 Prairie Lake Court
Aurora, IL 60504
630-978-2500
www.berninausa.com

The Warm Company

Batting
5529 186th Place SW
Lynnwood, WA 98037
425-248-2424
www.warmcompany.com

Willow Leaf Studio Designs

Pantographs
Willow Leaf Studio
P.O. Box 509
Montrose, BC V0G 1P0
Canada
888-945-5695
www.jodibeamish.com
www.willowleafstudio.com